An Alphabet of
DINOSAURS

An Alphabet of

DINOSAURS

BY PETER DODSON • PAINTINGS BY WAYNE D. BARLOWE

Black-and-white illustrations by Michael Meaker

A BYRON PREISS VISUAL PUBLICATIONS, INC. BOOK

For Cayley Samantha Barlowe.
From the start, this was always your book.
With all my love for you, forever.

—W.D.B.

To all the children who let me teach them something.
You don't know how much it means to me.

—P.D.

Designed by Dean Motter
Edited by Howard Zimmerman
Paintings copyright © 1995 by Wayne D. Barlowe
Line art copyright © 1995 by Michael Meaker

Library of Congress Cataloging-in-Publication Data

Dodson, Peter.
    An alphabet of dinosaurs / by Peter Dodson : illustrated by Wayne Barlowe.
        p.   cm.
    "A Byron Preiss book."
    ISBN 0-590-46486-8
    1. Dinosaurs—Juvenile literature. [1. Dinosaurs.] I. Barlowe, Wayne Douglas, ill. II. Title.
    QE862.D5D63 1995
    567.9'1—dc   94-15522

12 11 10 9 8 7 6 5 4 3 2 1   5 6 7 8 9/9 0/0

Printed in Singapore

First printing, March 1995

ABOUT THIS BOOK

IT HAS BEEN MORE THAN 60 MILLION YEARS since dinosaurs roamed the earth, but our fascination with these prehistoric creatures has never disappeared. Scientists around the world search for and study dinosaur fossils. These studies are constantly teaching us new facts about dinosaurs. We now know that dinosaurs lived on all of Earth's continents. Dinosaur fossils have been found from Alaska to Antarctica!

The 26 dinosaurs in this book are just a tiny portion of the many different kinds of dinosaurs that lived during the 150 million years known as the Mesozoic Era. We have included dinosaurs from all three periods of the Mesozoic: the Triassic Period (from 245 million years ago until 205 million years ago), the Jurassic Period (from 205 million years ago until 140 million years ago), and the Cretaceous Period (from 140 million years ago to 65 million years ago). Some of the dinosaurs that appear here will be very familiar. Some of these dinosaurs have been discovered only in the past few years.

The paintings in this book show the dinosaurs as we now think of them. Gone is the image of slow-moving giants. Gone is the picture of tail-dragging lizards. Instead, we see vibrant, active dinosaurs living in a world filled with brightly colored animals and plants. It is our hope that the images and information in this book will give you a greater appreciation for the monsters of the Mesozoic.

Ankylosaurus was a well-protected dinosaur. It had bony plates as tough as armor under its skin. Its clublike tail could knock over an animal the size of a horse.

Ankylosaurus had a heavy knob of bone at the end of its long tail. It defended itself from attackers by swinging its tail from side to side.

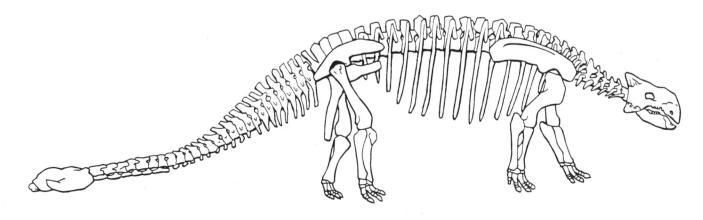

Baryonyx had a long, heavy curved claw on each of its front limbs. Fans of this meat eater have nicknamed it "claws."

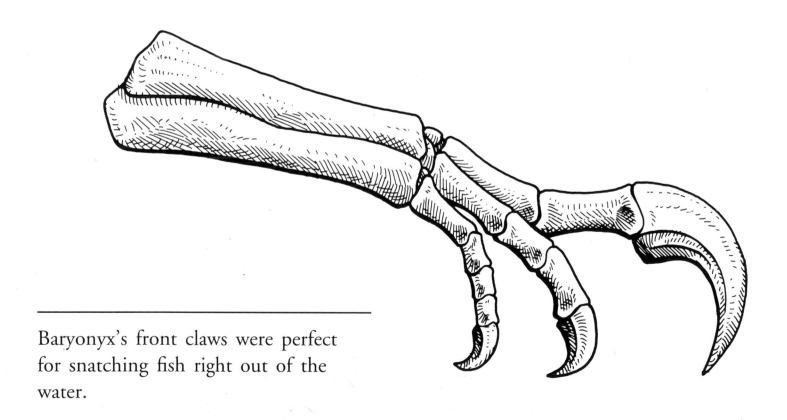

Baryonyx's front claws were perfect for snatching fish right out of the water.

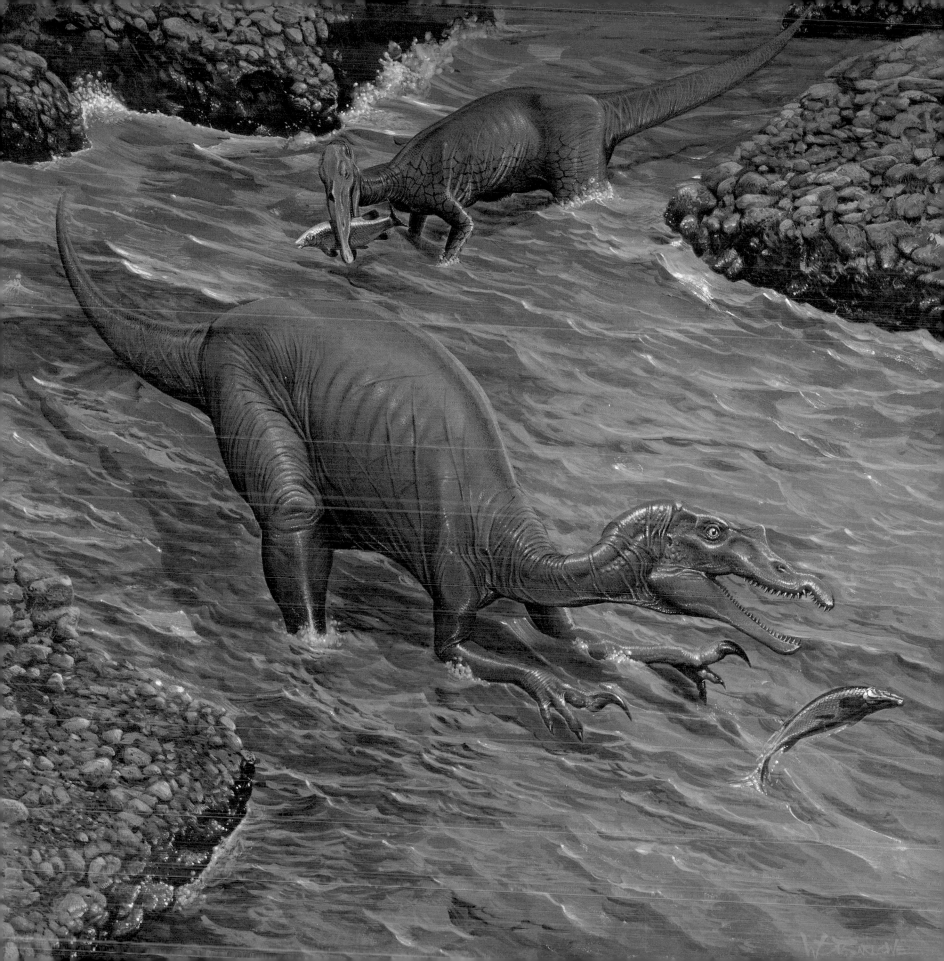

Chasmosaurus looked a lot like a smaller Triceratops. Like their larger cousins, Chasmosaurs traveled in great herds across North America.

Chasmosaurus used its birdlike beak to graze on ground plants as it moved with the herd.

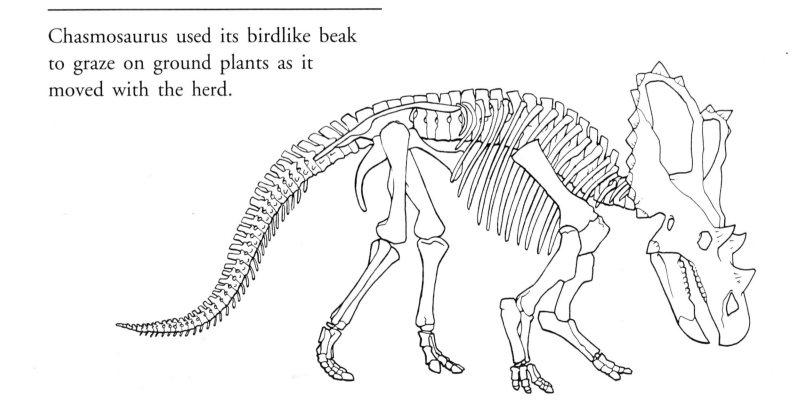

Deinonychus used its sharp claws as weapons. Some scientists think it may have balanced on one foot and its tail while it attacked with the claws on its other foot. Other scientists guess that Deinonychus may have leaped on its victims with both claws extended.

Deinonychus was a fast-moving dinosaur. It had a larger brain than many other dinosaurs alive at that time, and it probably hunted in packs.

Erlikosaurus was ten feet long and not built for speed. Scientists believe it moved very slowly.

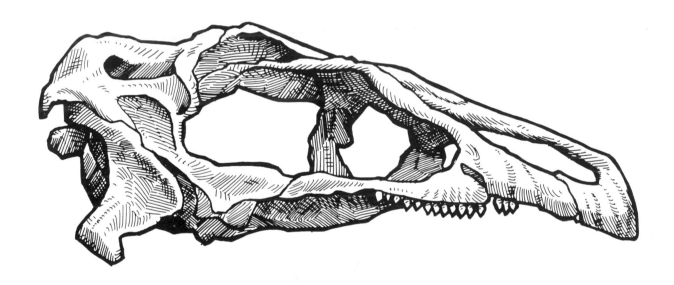

Erlikosaurus probably lived on insects. Like modern anteaters, its claws would have been useful for tearing open rotten trees and termite nests.

F abrosaurus was one of the earliest dinosaurs. It was a small, two-legged animal, and thought to be a fast runner.

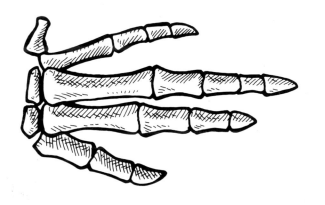

Fabrosaurus was about a foot tall and three feet long. Many of today's dogs are larger than this prehistoric creature.

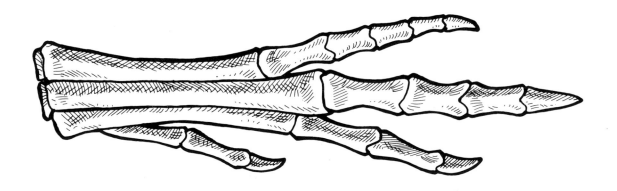

G

allimimus looked like an ostrich, but with arms instead of wings. Like the ostrich, Gallimimus ran as fast as a racehorse.

Gallimimus held its tail straight out for balance when it walked or ran. It had a beak with no teeth, just as birds do today.

Herrerasaurus is one of the oldest-known dinosaurs. This early meat eater was an ancestor of Tyrannosaurus rex. It used its many sharp teeth to devour lizardlike creatures.

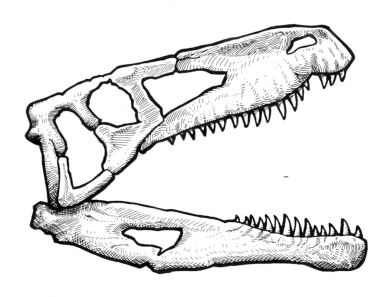

Herrerasaurs grew up to 18 feet long. Each of its arms had three long, curved fingers, and two smaller, stubby ones.

Iguanodon had spikes on its front limbs where other animals have thumbs. But the first Iguanodon fossil was found with only one unattached spike. Scientists thought it belonged on the end of the dinosaur's nose, like a rhinoceros's horn.

Iguanodon was as big as a large elephant. It probably ran on two legs for speed, but walked along on four.

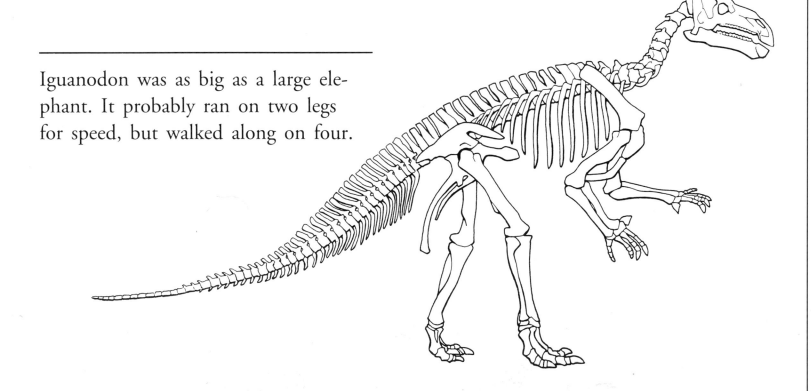

Janenschia was part of a group of long-necked plant eaters called Titanosaurs. These animals could move their tails easily in all directions.

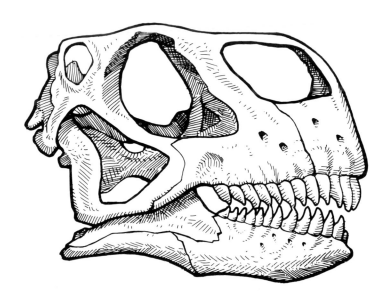

Janenschia was able to eat leaves from high up on trees, making good use of its long neck. It spent most of its waking time eating.

K

entrosaurus, like its cousin Stegosaurus, could swing its spiky tail as a weapon when it was in danger.

Kentrosaurus had a sharp beak for biting off plants, and lots of sharp spikes to protect itself from meat-eating dinosaurs.

Leptoceratops was a tiny, distant cousin of Triceratops. Since its front legs were so much shorter than its back legs, some scientists think it may have run on its long hind limbs.

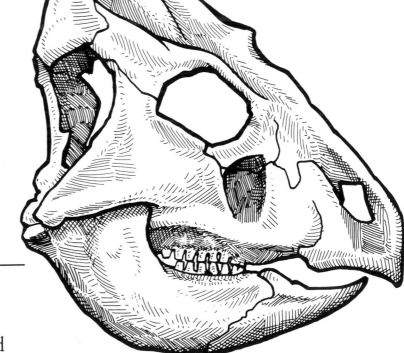

Leptoceratops was a small dinosaur. When it was fully grown, it measured only six feet long and weighed about 120 pounds.

Maiasaura mothers laid their eggs in nests built of leaves and other plant matter. They brought food to their babies and protected them until they were big enough to leave the nest.

Maiasaura was a hadrosaur, which is a group of dinosaurs that had flat beaks. They are also called "duckbilled dinosaurs."

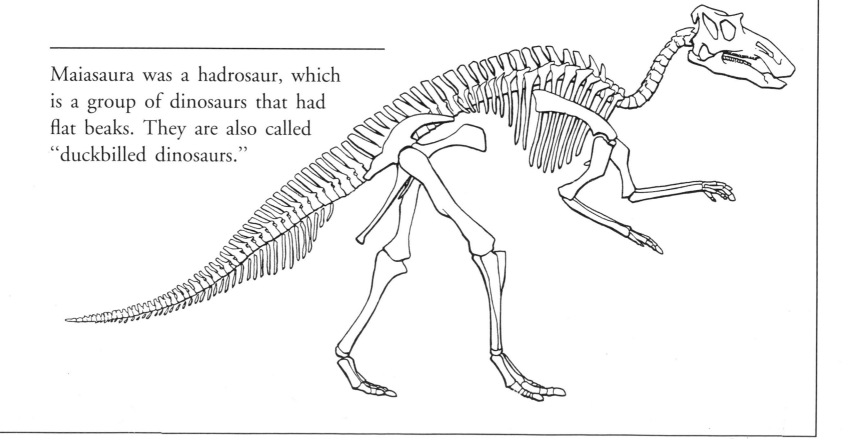

Nanotyrannus was a small-size cousin to Tyrannosaurus rex. It was a meat eater and an excellent hunter.

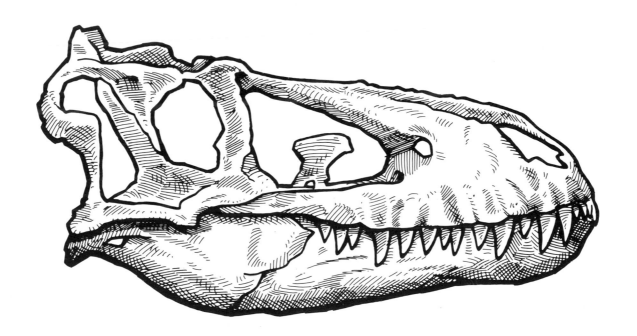

Nanotyrannus had lots of sharp teeth and excellent vision. These helped make it a dangerous hunter.

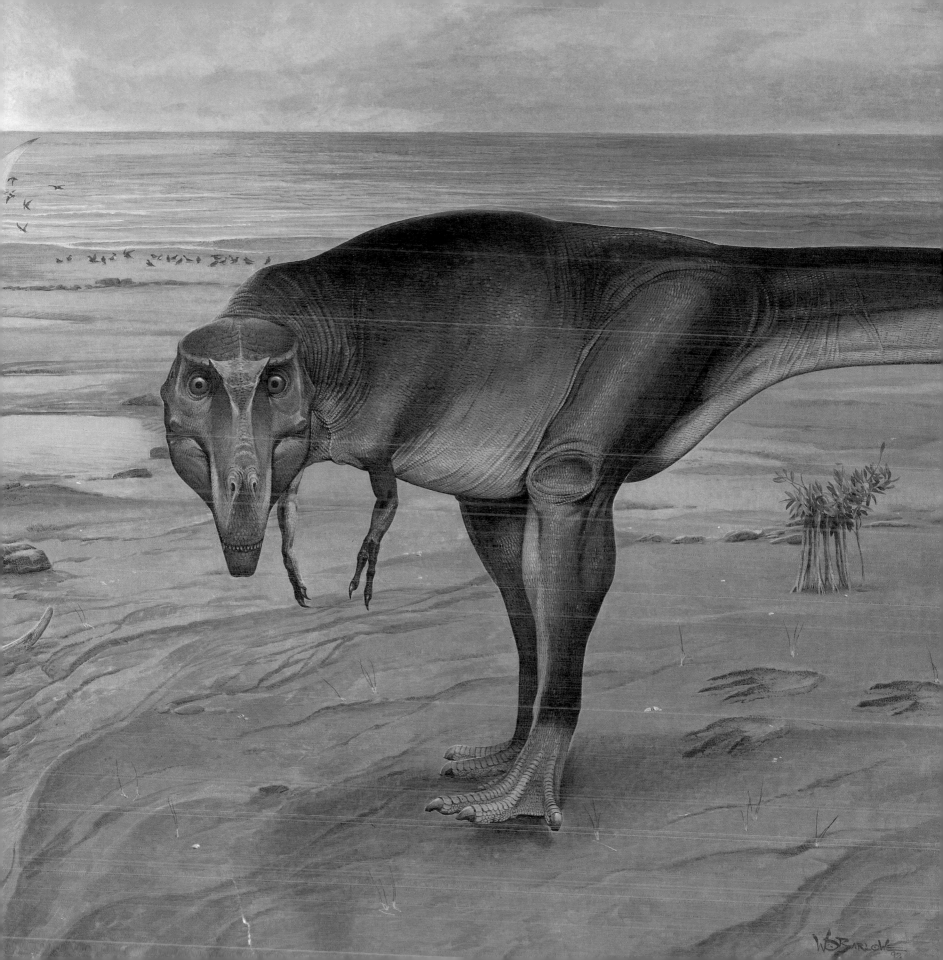

Oviraptor fossils have been found near ancient seashores. They probably caught and ate crabs and other kinds of shellfish. Oviraptors also may have eaten eggs stolen from dinosaur and reptile nests.

Oviraptors had no teeth, but they had powerful beaks. They used their beaks to crack open the shells of their meals.

Pentaceratops males fought to see which one was strongest. They locked their huge horns and pushed and shoved at each other. But they usually stopped before either one was badly hurt.

Pentaceratops was one of the largest of the horned dinosaurs. Its five sharp horns and huge frill were used as weapons and for protection.

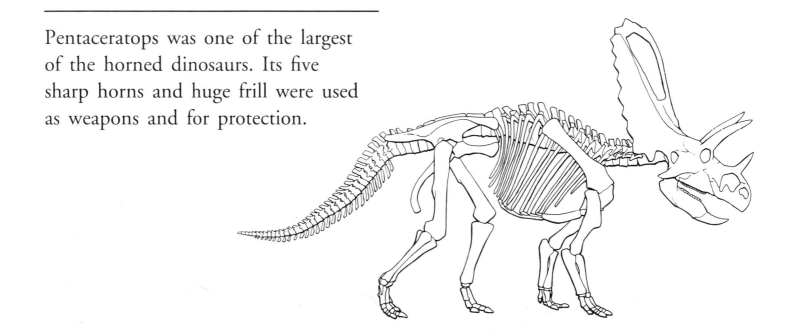

Quaesitosaurus was related to the giant American plant eaters. Its cousins include Apatosaurus (you may know it as Brontosaurus) and Diplodocus.

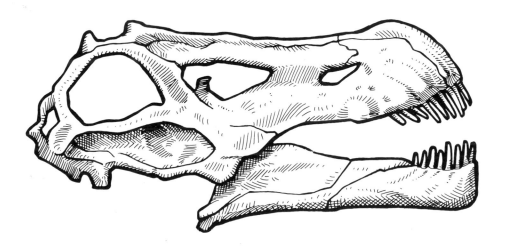

Scientists have been able to find only one Quaesitosaurus skull, but they have determined that the dinosaur was a large, long-necked plant eater.

Riojasaurus walked on four legs, but its long neck made it easy for this dinosaur to eat leaves from high in the trees. At times it may have stood on its rear legs and tail to reach food.

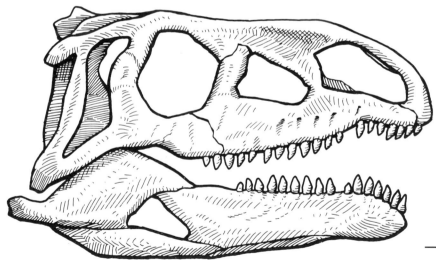

Riojasaurus (opposite, below) was a dinosaur with long, thick legs and a small head. But its most interesting feature was its teeth. This plant eater had sharp fangs, just like a meat eater.

Stegosaurus had triangular
back plates, along with spikes on
its tail, which probably served as
good protection.

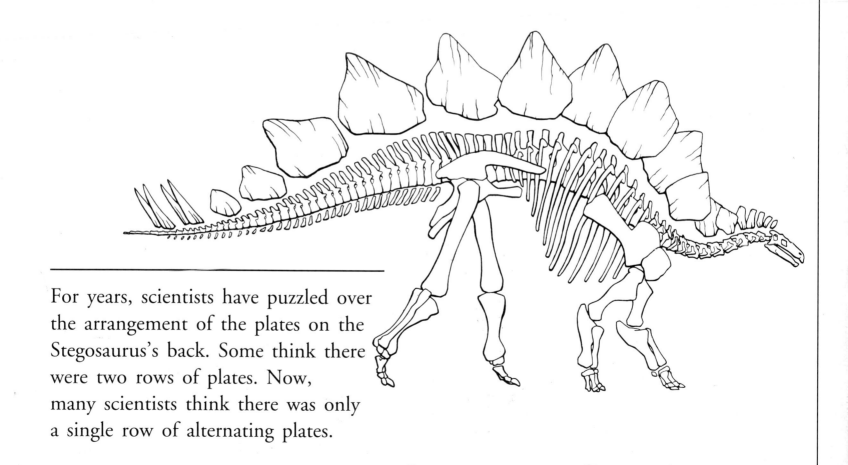

For years, scientists have puzzled over
the arrangement of the plates on the
Stegosaurus's back. Some think there
were two rows of plates. Now,
many scientists think there was only
a single row of alternating plates.

Tyrannosaurus was the greatest of all meat eaters. Scientists cannot agree on how this dinosaur captured its prey. Some believe it ran fast and chased down other animals. Others think the Tyrannosaurus rex may have moved slowly and eaten animals that were already dead.

This monster dinosaur's head was four and a half feet long, and the daggerlike teeth in its huge mouth were each half a foot long.

Ultrasauros was the giant among giants. This long-necked dinosaur was so tall that it could eat leaves from trees 55 feet high.

Ultrasauros is the largest dinosaur ever found. It may have been the largest animal ever to live on land. This monster was over 100 feet long, and weighed up to 150 tons.

Velociraptor was a speedy little meat eater. It attacked plant eaters that were up to five times larger than itself.

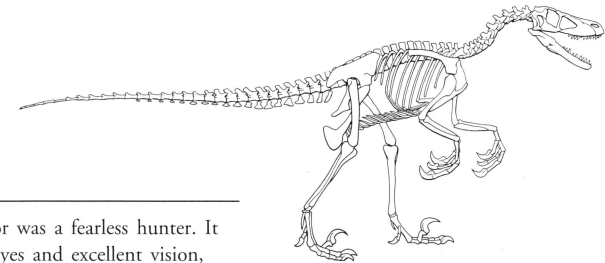

Velociraptor was a fearless hunter. It had large eyes and excellent vision, and may have hunted at night or twilight.

W
annanosaurus was a member of the family called "dome heads" or "bone heads." These dinosaurs had extra heavy skulls as round and thick as bowling balls.

Wannanosaurus was a tiny dinosaur that walked on two legs. It was a primitive "bone head." Later animals in this family had even thicker skulls.

X

enotarsosaurus was only recently discovered. The part of it that was most complete was a fossil leg. It was four feet long with an odd pattern of ankle bones. They were fused together, unlike the ankles of most other dinosaurs.

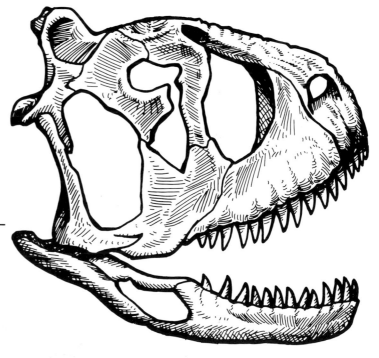

Xenotarsosaurus was a meat eater that walked on two legs, and was probably a swift runner. It may have been a distant cousin of Tyrannosaurus rex.

Yangchuanosaurus was a two-legged hunter. Its large jaws held saw-edged, daggerlike fangs for biting and holding its prey.

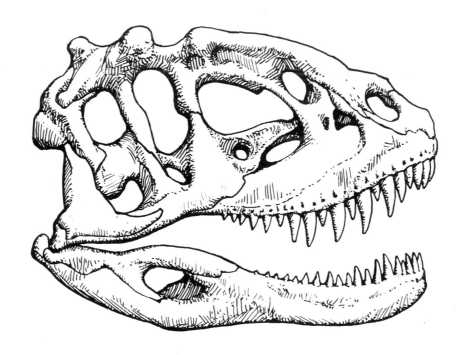

Yangchuanosaurus had powerful legs with large toe claws, and a long, heavy tail that it held straight out for balance.

Zephyrosaurus was a small, two-legged plant eater, but it was a swift runner.

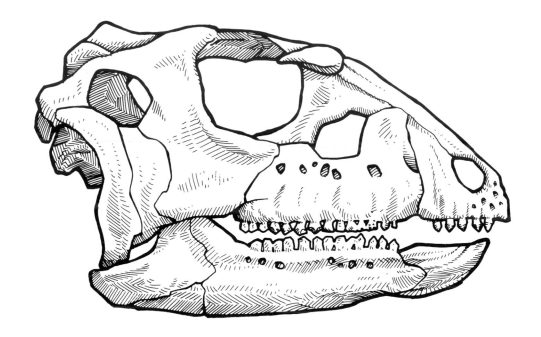

Zephyrosaurus was a member of the dinosaur family called Hypsilophodontids. They all had long legs and feet that were perfect for sprinting. This family has been nicknamed the "dinosaur gazelles."

A GUIDE TO THE DINOSAURS IN THIS BOOK

TRIASSIC PERIOD—FROM 245 MILLION YEARS AGO TO 205 MILLION YEARS AGO
JURASSIC PERIOD—FROM 205 MILLION YEARS AGO TO 140 MILLION YEARS AGO
CRETACEOUS PERIOD—FROM 140 MILLION YEARS AGO TO 65 MILLION YEARS AGO

ANKYLOSAURUS

(ANK-EE-low-SAW-rus)

What Its Name Means: Stiff lizard

What It Ate: Plants

When It Lived: The Late Cretaceous Period

Where Fossils Were Found: Western
    North America

Length: Up to 25 feet long

BARYONYX

(BAR-EE-on-ix)

What Its Name Means: Heavy claw

What It Ate: Meat

When It Lived: The Early Cretaceous Period

Where Fossils Were Found: England,
    Europe, and Niger, Africa

Length: Up to 30 feet long

CHASMOSAURUS

(KAZ-mo-SAW-rus)

What Its Name Means: Ravine reptile

What It Ate: Plants

When It Lived: The Late Cretaceous Period

Where Fossils Were Found: Western
    North America

Length: Up to 17 feet long

DEINONYCHUS

(DIE-no-NI-kus)

What Its Name Means: Terrible claw

What It Ate: Meat

When It Lived: The Early Cretaceous Period

Where Fossils Were Found: Western
    North America

Length: Up to 11 feet long

ERLIKOSAURUS

(er-LIK-oh-SAW-rus)

What Its Name Means: Erlik's lizard
    (After the Mongolian
    King of the Dead)

What It Ate: Meat

When It Lived: The Late Cretaceous Period

Where Fossils Were Found: Mongolia,
    East Asia

Length: Up to 12 feet long

FABROSAURUS

(FAB-ro-SAW-rus)

What Its Name Means: Fabre's lizard
    (Named after French
    geologist Jean Fabre)

What It Ate: Plants

When It Lived: The Early Jurassic Period

Where Fossils Were Found: South
    Africa, Africa

Length: Up to 4 feet long

GALLIMIMUS

(GAL-ih-MIME-us)

What Its Name Means: Chicken mimic

What It Ate: Plants and meat

When It Lived: The Late Cretaceous Period

Where Fossils Were Found: Mongolia,
    East Asia

Length: Up to 17 feet long

JANENSCHIA

(yah-NEN-shee-ah)

What Its Name Means: In honor of
    Wilhelm Janesch
    (A German paleontologist)

What It Ate: Plants

When It Lived: The Late Jurassic Period

Where Fossils Were Found: East
    Africa, Africa

Length: Up to 60 feet long

HERRERASAURUS

(HER-RARE-a-SAW-rus)

What Its Name Means: Herrera's lizard (To
    honor Don Victoria Herrera, a
    rancher from the region in Argen-
    tina where the fossils were
    found.)

What It Ate: Meat

When It Lived: The Late Triassic Period

Where Fossils Were Found: Argentina,
    South America

Length: Up to 18 feet long

KENTROSAURUS

(KEN-tro-SAW-rus)

What Its Name Means: Sharp-pointed lizard

What It Ate: Plants

When It Lived: The Late Jurassic Period

Where Fossils Were Found: East
    Africa, Africa

Length: Up to 17 feet long

IGUANODON

(ig-WA-no-DON)

What Its Name Means: Iguana tooth

What It Ate: Plants

When It Lived: The Early Cretaceous Period

Where Fossils Were Found: Europe and Asia

Length: Up to 25 feet long

LEPTOCERATOPS

(LEP-toh-SER-a-tops)

What Its Name Means: Slender horn face

What It Ate: Plants

When It Lived: The Early Cretaceous Period

Where Fossils Were Found: Western
    North America

Length: Up to 6 feet long

MAIASAURA

(MY-a-SAW-ra)

What Its Name Means: Good mother reptile

What It Ate: Plants

When It Lived: The Late Cretaceous Period

Where Fossils Were Found: Montana,
United States

Length: Up to 30 feet long

NANOTYRANNUS

(NAN-O-tie-RAN-us)

What Its Name Means: Tiny tyrant

What It Ate: Meat

When It Lived: The Late Cretaceous Period

Where Fossils Were Found: North America

Length: Up to 17 feet long

OVIRAPTOR

(ove-ih-RAP-tor)

What Its Name Means: Egg thief

What It Ate: Meat

When It Lived: The Late Cretaceous Period

Where Fossils Were Found: Mongolia,
East Asia

Length: Up to 6 feet long

PENTACERATOPS

(PEN-ta-SER-a-tops)

What Its Name Means: Five-horn face

What It Ate: Plants

When It Lived: The Late Cretaceous Period

Where Fossils Were Found: New
Mexico, United States

Length: Up to 20 feet long

QUAESITOSAURUS

(KAY-sit-o-SAW-rus)

What Its Name Means: Uncommon reptile
(So named because of a strange
bony tube in its skull)

What It Ate: Plants

When It Lived: The Late Cretaceous Period

Where Fossils Were Found: Mongolia,
East Asia

Length: Up to 50 feet long

RIOJASAURUS

(REE-OH-ha-SAW-rus)

What Its Name Means: Lizard from Rioja
(a province of Argentina)

What It Ate: Plants

When It Lived: The Late Triassic Period

Where Fossils Were Found: Argentina,
South America

Length: Up to 36 feet long

STEGOSAURUS

(STEG-o-SAW-rus)

What Its Name Means: Plated reptile

What It Ate: Plants

When It Lived: The Late Jurassic Period

Where Fossils Were Found: Western United
States, North America

Length: Up to 25 feet long

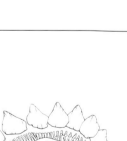

TYRANNOSAURUS REX

(tie-RAN-o-saw-rus rex)

What Its Name Means: Tyrant lizard

What It Ate: Meat

When It Lived: The Late Cretaceous Period

Where Fossils Were Found: Western North
America and People's Republic
of China, East Asia

Length: Up to 40 feet long

ULTRASAUROS

(UL-tra-SAW-ros)

What Its Name Means: Lizard beyond others

What It Ate: Plants

When It Lived: The Late Jurassic Period

Where Fossils Were Found: North America

Length: Up to 100 feet long

VELOCIRAPTOR

(vel-AH-see-RAP-tor)

What Its Name Means: Swift thief

What It Ate: Meat

When It Lived: The Late Cretaceous Period

Where Fossils Were Found: Mongolia,
People's Republic of China, and
Kazakhstan, East Asia

Length: Up to 6 feet long

WANNANOSAURUS

(wahn-NAN-o-SAW-rus)

What Its Name Means: Lizard from south-
ern Anhui Province

What It Ate: Plants

When It Lived: The Late Cretaceous Period

Where Fossils Were Found: People's
Republic of China, East Asia

Length: Up to 5 feet long

XENOTARSOSAURUS

(ZEEN-o-TAR-so-SAW-rus)

What Its Name Means: Strange ankle lizard

What It Ate: Meat

When It Lived: The Late Cretaceous Period

Where Fossils Were Found: Argentina,
South America

Length: Up to 12 feet long

YANGCHUANOSAURUS

(YANG-chew-an-o-SAW-rus)

What Its Name Means: Lizard from
Yangchuan County

What It Ate: Meat

When It Lived: The Late Jurassic Period

Where Fossils Were Found: People's
Republic of China, East Asia

Length: Up to 33 feet long

ZEPHYROSAURUS

(zef-EAR-roe-SAW-rus)

What Its Name Means: West wind lizard

What It Ate: Plants

When It Lived: The Early Cretaceous Period

Where Fossils Were Found: Western United
States, North America

Length: Up to 6 feet long

WHAT HAPPENED TO THE DINOSAURS?

EVERYONE KNOWS THAT THE DINOSAURS died out (or became extinct) about 65 million years ago. Does this mean that the dinosaurs were failures? No! Most plants and animals that have ever lived are extinct.

Our study of the fossil record shows that most kinds of animals only live for a certain amount of time. Most mammals that are extinct lived for 1 or 2 million years. Some kinds of snails and clams lived for 10 to 12 million years before becoming extinct.

Dinosaurs survived for 160 million years, making them far more successful than human animals, who have only been around for about 2 million years. Dinosaur families were constantly going extinct. Over that 160-million-year period, the dinosaurs that lived on Earth changed completely 30 times!

Herrerasaurus, which lived 225 million years ago, had been extinct for 75 million years before Stegosaurs appeared. And Stegosaurs were extinct for nearly 85 million years before Tyrannosaurs appeared. Tyrannosaurs, along with Triceratops and Edmontosaurs, were among the last dinosaurs on Earth. But in one sense dinosaurs are not extinct at all, because their genetic material lives on in birds. In fact, some dinosaur scientists now consider that birds *are* dinosaurs!

We always want to say why something became extinct even though we almost never know for sure. Scientists have many different ideas about why the dinosaurs became extinct. The most exciting idea is that a comet or asteroid—maybe as large as six miles wide—smashed into the earth 65 million years ago. The impact would have formed a crater 100 miles across. Clouds of dust would have circled the globe, causing temperatures to drop. Storms and wildfires would have swept around the world, causing darkness that would have lasted for months. Lower temperatures might have brought freezing weather that could have killed the dinosaurs. Most of the plants on Earth would have died without sunlight, and only their seeds would have survived.

But other scientists believe that explosions of several large volcanoes could have caused the same kinds of conditions. They think the extinction of the dinosaurs can be explained without supposing that a comet smashed into the planet. Still other scientists think that a comet combined with volcanic explosions was the cause of the dinosaurs' extinction.

Whatever caused the catastrophe of 65 million years ago, not all animals died out. Many survived after the dinosaurs were gone. Sharks, bony fish, frogs, turtles, crocodiles, lizards, and mammals spread across the earth and thrived. This has led some scientists to think that the extinction of the dinosaurs may have happened more slowly, perhaps due to a change in climate.

The climate had been very warm for most of the dinosaurs' long reign, but started to cool a little toward the end. Perhaps this saved the smaller animals, who could seek refuge or hibernate. And, since water temperature changes far more slowly than air temperature, perhaps this saved the sharks and other marine animals. Some scientists think that the dinosaurs became extinct because they couldn't adjust to new forms of plant life, or that diseases killed off whole populations. But we may never find the evidence to say if these theories are right or wrong. The sad fact is, we may never know for sure just what killed off the dinosaurs.

Dr. Peter Dodson

Dr. Peter Dodson is a professor of anatomy at the University of Pennsylvania. He is also the vice president and head of the book review committee of The Dinosaur Society.

Dr. Dodson has written two other dinosaur books for kids—*Giant Dinosaurs* and *Baby Dinosaurs*, both published in 1990 by Scholastic Inc. He was the editor of the 1990 book, *The Dinosauria,* one of the best books ever written on the subject. He discovered Avaceratops, the smallest cousin of Triceratops, on a dig in Montana in 1986. Dr. Dodson currently lives with his family in Philadelphia.

Wayne D. Barlowe

Wayne D. Barlowe's love of art, nature, and the natural world comes from his parents. They are both longtime artists and have illustrated many natural-history guides. When he began his art education at the Cooper Union, he also began an apprenticeship at the American Museum of Natural History in New York City.

As a professional, he has painted over 300 covers for science-fiction books. His first book, *Barlowe's Guide to Extraterrestrials*, was published by Workman Publishing in 1979. It is a natural-history guide to some of the most famous aliens in science fiction. A second book, *Expedition,* focuses on the strange animal life found on an alien world. It was published in 1990 by Workman. Barlowe currently lives in New Jersey with his wife and two daughters.

Michael Meaker

Michael Meaker has been a staff illustrator for the Natural History Museum of Los Angeles since graduating from art school in 1988. He was the primary illustrator for the book *Sharks: Fact and Fantasy,* published by the Natural History Museum of Los Angeles.

He contributed several paintings to *The Ultimate Dinosaur,* published in 1992 by Bantam Books. He has also illustrated a book and an exhibit on whales for the Natural History Museum of Los Angeles, and has done illustrations for several exhibits at the Los Angeles Zoo. Meaker currently lives in South Pasadena and is hard at work on several new dinosaur projects.